Bill of Rights
FOR KIDS
(for use in schools)

We the People

I work for YOU!

Karen Moran

Illustrated by Nicole Easter

Bill of Rights for Kids *(for use in schools)*
Book 2 in the Founding Documents for Kids series

Karen Moran books may be ordered through https://Karen-Moran.com, book sellers or by contacting:

Published by:
Patriot Country Publishers
https:/PatriotCountryPublishers.com
info@PatriotCountryPublishers.com

Karen Moran
P. O. Box 210384
Royal Palm Beach, FL 33421

Illustrations and graphics by Nicole Easter:
createdinhisimagestudios.com

Because of the dynamic nature of the internet, any web addresses or links contained in this book may have changed since publication and may no longer be valid. The views expressed in this book are solely the views of the author.

ISBN-13: 979-8-9881303-1-4
Library of Congress Control Number: 2025907558
Printed in the United States of America.

Authors Thoughts

On July 4, 2026 the United States celebrates the 250th Anniversary of its founding which was July 4, 1776. With events that have occurred since the Presidential Election of 2016, many believe we are in the process of restoring our nation to the Founding Fathers' original intent.

The following famous excerpt from our Declaration of Independence reads:

> We hold these truths to be self-evident, that all men are created equal, that they are endowed by their Creator with certain unalienable rights, that among these are life, liberty and the pursuit of happiness. That to secure these rights, governments are instituted among men, deriving their just powers from the consent of the governed.

When the Constitution was written, many of the Founding Fathers were unhappy, wanting it to include a Bill of Rights to protect the people from abuse by their government. Having experienced their rights greatly trampled upon by the British, their intent was for their new government to work for the people and protect their rights.

This book helps people learn what is in the Constitution and the Bill of Rights. By being knowledgeable of our Constitutional rights, we will know when they are violated and be better prepared to defend these rights, protect our freedom, and the freedom of future generations.

- Karen Moran

Introduction to the Bill of Rights

The Bill of Rights was added to the original U.S. Constitution drafted in Philadelphia, PA at the Constitutional Convention. The reason the Bill of Rights was so important to the people was that they had 27 grievances against the British government. These 27 grievances were all stated in the Declaration of Independence of 1776. Because the British would not listen to the colonies and address their 27 concerns, the colonists broke away from the British government and fought the American Revolutionary War. They freed themselves from the tyranny of the British empire.

After The U.S. Constitution was written there were three months of debate and some states and individuals did not want to sign the U.S. Constitution into law without serious additions to address their 27 grievances they had had with the British Empire. Of the 55 delegates at the convention, a total of 39 signed the document. Many were suspicious that a federal government would try to control them like the British had done. George Mason was among those that refused to sign unless a Bill of Rights was added to the Constitution.

What year was the U.S. Constitution signed? It was on September 17th, 1787. It needed to then be ratified (signed into law) by 9 of the 13 states before it could be law. It took a while for the states to agree to ratify it.

For the signing of the Constitution to gain popularity among the people, James Madison, Alexander Hamilton, and John Jay wrote a series of essays to persuade people to ratify the Constitution. These 85 essays became known as The Federalist Papers. People who supported the Constitution became known as Federalists while those opposed became known as Anti-Federalists.

After the 9th state of New Hampshire finally ratified the Constitution, it became law on June 21, 1788. During the 1st Congress, on September 25, 1789, 12

Amendments were proposed by James Madison and added to the Constitution. The first 10 Amendments became known as The Bill of Rights.

TABLE OF CONTENTS

SECTION ONE:
Bill of Rights
The First 10 Amendments

SECTION TWO:
Catechism (Trivia)

SECTION THREE:
Founding Fathers Hall of Fame

SECTION FOUR:
Additional Historic Documents

Bill of Rights: First Ten Amendments

Amendment 1

FREEDOM OF RELIGION, SPEECH, PRESS, RIGHT TO ASSEMBLE PEACEABLY AND TO PETITION THE GOVERNMENT

AMENDMENT 1

Congress cannot establish a national religion like other countries have or take away the right of the people to exercise their religion freely. The people also have freedom of speech, freedom of the press (media) and the right to peaceably assemble and petition the government to make things right if it has caused them harm.

Note: the original wording for Amendments 1-10 are on pages 79-84

Amendment 1

Amendment 1 contains 5 different rights that people felt they needed protection for.

1. Freedom of Religion

2. Freedom of Speech

3. Freedom of the Press

4. The Right to Assemble Peaceably

5. The Right to Petition the Government (to redress grievances and make things right.)

Can you name these five rights?

<u>Think about it-Discuss</u>

Which of these rights do you feel have been violated and why?

Has anyone you know been kept from freely expressing their political or religious opinion?

Have you heard of anyone going to jail for their religious or political opinion?

Do you feel that there has been any censoring of information on social media, news channels or where people work?

Amendment 2

THE RIGHT TO BEAR ARMS

AMENDMENT 2

People have the right to keep and bear arms and form a civilian military force if necessary. Taking away people's arms (guns, etc.) is not authorized by the Constitution, and this right shall not be violated.

Original wording for this Amendment is on page 81.

Amendment 2

Amendment 2 is about the right to keep and bear arms. Arms are weapons of offense or defense and include ammunition. The word *arms* can include a wide range of weapons suitable to their conditions and as allowed by law. People wanted it to be stated in the Constitution that people have the right to keep and carry a gun for individual self-defense. They did not exclude additional weapons such as those needed to form a civilian military force. A civilian military force was what was needed by the colonies in the American Revolutionary War to defeat the British government. The British government had wanted to take away the guns that belonged to the colonies so the colonies would have no way to defend themselves. By having the right to bear arms, the newly formed Republic wanted to ensure that their newly formed federal government would not oppress or punish them for unjust reasons.

Think About It-Discuss

Do you feel that people should be allowed to have guns for self-defense?

Have some people misused the privilege of owning a gun?

How can the use of guns be made safe?

Amendment 3

THE HOUSING OF SOLDIERS

AMENDMENT 3

A soldier cannot stay in a citizen's home without their consent. In time of war, a soldier may only stay in a citizen's home if a law passed by Congress says he can.

Original wording for this Amendment is on page 81.

Amendment 3

This amendment was written because the British empire forced the colonists to allow British soldiers to stay in their homes and to feed them.

The colonists felt that it was unfair that they should be forced to do this.

This was only one of many things the colonists felt were unfair.

Think about it-Discuss

How would you feel if the government forced you to have uninvited people stay in your home and make you feed them at your own expense?

Can you think of anything your own government has forced people to do that was against what they felt was right or fair?

Have you ever been forced in school to learn information that you felt was false?

Amendment 4

PROTECTION FROM UNREASONABLE SEARCHES AND SEIZURES

AMENDMENT 4

A person's home or personal property cannot be unreasonably searched without a warrant (written document) believing a crime has been committed and describing what is to be searched for and taken.

Can anyone think of a case where this Amendment was violated?

Original wording for this Amendment is on page 82.

Amendment 4

British Army officers would often search through the homes of the colonists looking for violations of their laws. The colonists were forced to buy goods with a stamp on them from the British, often at higher prices. If the British found items in their homes without a stamp on them, the colonists were punished.

Think about it-Discuss

How would you feel if the police could come into your house and search through your home and take anything they wanted?

Do you think this ever happened even to a former President of a country?

Should the colonists have been able to purchase items wherever they wanted?

Do you think there is ever a time a person should not be able to purchase an item?

Amendment 5

PROTECTION OF RIGHTS TO LIFE, LIBERTY AND PROPERTY

AMENDMENT 5

The following definition for an indictment by a Grand jury is from the: American Dictionary of English Language - Noah Webster 1828.

1. A written accusation or formal charge of a crime or misdemeanor, referred by a grand jury under oath to a court. Blackstone.

2. The paper or parchment containing the accusation of a grand jury.

Original wording for this Amendment is on page 82.

Amendment 5

This Amendment is a laundry list of our protections against criminal prosecution. It includes the right to remain silent. It also includes the right for compensation for property takenand used by the government.

In addition, it includes the right to due process. So what is "*due process*" of law? The due process of law is a fundamental principle of fairness that protects citizens from the government by ensuring that all legal procedures are followed. It is a safeguard to protect the life, liberty, and property from being taken without fair process. It protects citizens from arbitrary or unreasonable government decisions.

The phrase *due process* of law first appeared in 1354 in the Magna Carta.

Think about it-Discuss

Why is it fairer to have a jury trial where your peers decide if you are guilty or innocent?

Should a person on trial be able to have

witnesses come forth to prove their innocence? If so, why?

Can you think of when it is okay for the government to pay you for your property and use it for the public good?

Amendment 6

RIGHTS OF ACCUSED PERSONS IN CRIMINAL CASES

AMENDMENT 6

Persons accused of a crime have a right to a speedy and public trial. They must be told of the charges against them. They have the right to have a lawyer. They have the right to question any accusers.

Original wording for this Amendment is on page 83.

Amendment 6

1. The 6th Amendment guarantees your right to have a speedy and a public trial by an impartial jury of the state or district where you have been charged with a crime.

2. You have the right to know of what crime you've been accused.

3. You have the right to confront your accusers and bring your own witnesses forward to challenge them.

4. You also have the right to an attorney to assist you in your defense.

Think about it-Discuss

1. Did the people accused of the United States Capitol Riot on January 6th, 2021, get a speedy trial?

2. Were they treated fairly?

3. What would happen if an accused person were not allowed to speak in their own defense or bring their own witnesses?

Amendment 7

RIGHTS IN CIVIL CASES

AMENDMENT 7

In most cases a person sued in a civil case has a right to a jury trial.

Original wording for this Amendment is on page 83.

Amendment 7

1. This Amendment guarantees your right to a jury trial in certain civil lawsuits under *common law* especially where major amounts of money are involved.

2. No fact tried by a jury can be re-examined except if they are examined by rules of *common law.*

***Common law* is a body of unwritten rules and principles received from our ancestors and universally accepted for a long time.

<u>Think about it-Discuss</u>

Where might the *common law* (also known as moral law) come from?

What main countries did the colonists come from?

Did they bring with them their religious beliefs?

Amendment 8

EXCESSIVE BAIL, FINES, AND PUNISHMENT FORBIDDEN

AMENDMENT 8

The Government cannot charge excessive bail, or fines, or inflict cruel and unusual punishment upon people.

Original wording for this Amendment is on page 84.

Amendment 8

1. In Amendment 8 you have the right to be free from excessive bail. (Bail is money or property given to ensure an arrested person will appear in court as directed.) Defendants must post bail to be released from custody until their trial.

2. In Amendment 8 you are also free from excessive fines.

3. Additionally, you are free from cruel and unusual punishment such as torture.

Think about it-Discuss

Why do you think the new Republican government was so concerned that their rights be protected?

What rights were people deprived of when they were under British rule? (see a list of 27 grievances listed in the Declaration of Independence)

Can you think about a time when this Amendment was violated? If so, what were the defendants denied?

What rights were violated in persons charged with the U.S. Capital Attack on January 6, 2021?

Amendment 9

MOST RIGHTS ARE KEPT BY THE PEOPLE

AMENDMENT 9

Many rights of the people are listed in the Constitution. Just because every right may not be listed, it does not mean other rights may be denied or kept from the people.

Original wording for this Amendment is on page 84.

1. Most rights are kept by the people. Your rights belong to you, not the government. Therefore, most rights are retained by the people.

2. The powers given to the federal government are listed (enumerated).

3. The powers that government does not have are also listed.

4. Just because every right may not be listed, does not mean other natural rights may be denied or kept from the people.

5. The people wanted to make sure that just because a right is not listed in the Constitution, it does not mean it is not a protected right of the people.

Think about it-Discuss

1. Who has the most rights, the people or the government?

2. Do all the rights of the people have to be listed in the Constitution?

3. What does enumerated mean?

Amendment 10

THE U.S. GOVERNMENT HAS LIMITED POWERS

AMENDMENT 10

The only powers that the United States government has are listed in the Constitution. All other rights are reserved to the states or to the people.

Original wording for this Amendment is on page 84.

Amendment 10

1. Powers not in the Constitution belong to the states or the people and are kept and reserved by and for the people.

2. There are some rights listed that the federal government has.

3. There are some rights listed that the states have.

4. All other rights belong to the people.

5. The Bill of Rights were added to the U.S. Constitution to address heated debates and because the Founding Fathers recognized the need to protect individual liberties from possible overreach by the federal government.

6. The Founding Fathers and the people wanted the government to always remember that the government works for them and should be their servant.

Think about it-Discuss

Do you think our government serves the people today?

Can you think of any ways the government has abused its power?

How do you think our government could improve to be a better servant of the people?

Bill of Rights
Catechism
(Trivia)

Bill of Rights Catechism (Trivia)

Question 1:

What is the Bill of Rights?

The Bill of Rights are the first 10 Amendments (changes) to the U.S. Constitution and list freedoms for Americans.

Question 2:

How many Amendments are in the Bill of Rights?

There are 10 Amendments listed in the Bill of Rights.

Question 3:

Why did certain Founding Fathers insist on the Bill of Rights?

Many Founding Father's insisted on the Bill of Rights to assure the citizens that their government would be limited, and the Government could not trample on the rights of the people.

Question 4:

What is the 1st Amendment about?

The 1st Amendment is about 5 rights that people have. The rights are: a) the right to exercise their religion freely; b) freedom of speech; c) freedom of the press; d) the right to assemble peaceably, and e) the right to petition the government to redress grievances and make things right.

Question 5:

What is the 2nd Amendment about?

The 2nd Amendment is about people having the right to keep and bear arms and form a civilian military force if necessary. Taking away people's arms (guns, etc.) is not authorized by the Constitution and this right shall not be violated.

Question 6:

What is the 3rd Amendment about?

The 3rd Amendment protects citizens from having soldiers stay in their homes without their consent. In time of war, a soldier may only stay in a citizen's home if a law passed by Congress says he can.

Question 7:

What is the 4th Amendment about?

The 4th Amendment states that a person's home or personal property cannot be unreasonably searched without a warrant (written document) believing a crime has been committed and describing what is to be searched for and taken.

Question 8:

What is the 5th Amendment about?

The 5th Amendment is all about the protection of people's rights to life, liberty, and property. a) If a person is accused of a serious crime punishable by death, they have a right to a jury trial. b) They do not have to testify against themselves. c) If a person's property is needed for public use, they must be paid fairly for it.

Question 9:

What is the 6th Amendment about?

The 6th Amendment says if a person is accused of a crime:

a) They have the right to a speedy and public trial.

b) They must be told charges against them and know who accuses them.

c) They have the right to have a lawyer.

d) They have the right to question any accusers.

Question 10:

What is the 7th Amendment about?

The 7th Amendment is about rights in a civil trial. Any fact proven by a jury cannot be examined in court again.

Question 11:

What is the 8th Amendment about?

The 8th Amendment says the Government cannot charge excessive bail, or fines, or inflict cruel and unusual punishment upon people.

Question 12:

What is the 9th Amendment about?

a) The 9th Amendment states most rights are kept by the people.

b) Many of those rights are listed in the Constitution.

c) Just because every right may not be listed, does not mean other natural rights may be denied or kept from the people.

Question 13:

What is the 10th Amendment about?

The 10th Amendment limits the powers of the U.S. Government. The only powers the U.S. Government has are listed in the Constitution. All other powers are reserved by the states or by the people.

Bonus Fun Question:

Which of the following is NOT a right listed by the Bill of Rights?

a) Right to free speech

b) Right to a fair trial

c) Right to own a pet

d) Right to practice any religion

Answer: c) Right to own a pet

Question 14

Who was called the Father of the Bill

of Rights?

George Mason was known as the Father of the Bill of Rights.

Question 15

How many states had to ratify the Constitution for it to become law in the nation?

According to Article 7 of the Constitution, 9 out of 13 states were needed to ratify the Constitution into law.

Question 16

Were all the 13 states eager to ratify the Constitution?

No, many did not feel the rights of the people were clearly protected in the

Constitution and that it needed a Bill of Rights.

Question 17

Who is Uncle Sam?

Uncle Sam is a fictional character to represent The United States government.

Question 18

Of the 55 delegates to the Constitutional Convention, why did some delegates not sign the Constitution?

Only 39 delegates would sign the Constitution because many were suspicious that a federal government would try to control them like the British had done.

Question 19

What were the papers circulated among the states to convince them to sign the Constitution?

The Federalist Papers were circulated between 1787-1788 to convince the states to sign the Constitution.

Question 20

Who were the three men responsible for writing the 85 essays known as The Federalist Papers?

The Federalist Papers were written by James Madison, Alexander Hamilton, and John Jay under the pseudonym of Publius.

Question 21

When did the Constitution become ratified?

The Constitution became law when it was ratified June 21st, 1788 by New Hampshire, the 9th state to ratify it.

Question 22

In Amendment 1 there is a statement that "Congress shall make no law respecting an establishment of religion or prohibiting the free exercise thereof". What does that mean?

In this Establishment Clause, it means that the government cannot establish its own religion. That is left up to the people. It also means that the government cannot prohibit (or stop) the free exercise of religion or religious speech.

Question 23

Why did the Establishment Clause matter so much to the people?

The Establishment Clause mattered to the people because the British tried to force them to accept their brand of Christianity only. They were persecuted for their beliefs and decided to come to America for freedom of religion. They wanted freedom *of* religion, not freedom *from* religion.

Question 24

Has there been any confusion in understanding the Establishment Clause in the 1st Amendment?

Yes, there is a phrase often quoted that says there is a "wall of separation between church and state."

Question 25

Who is responsible for the statement that says there is a "wall of separation" between church and state and where is this statement found?"

The statement was made in 1802 by then President Thomas Jefferson in a letter to the Danbury Baptist Church.

Question 26

Is the wording "wall of separation between church and state" found anywhere in any of our founding documents?

No, this wording is not found anywhere in the Declaration of Independence, the Constitution or The Bill of Rights.

Question 27

Why did President Thomas Jefferson write a letter to the Danbury Baptist Church?

President Thomas Jefferson wrote the Danbury Baptist Association to ensure them that they would not be persecuted for their "brand of Christianity" because there was a "wall of separation between church and state".

See Letter to the Danbury Baptists on pages 85-88.

Question 28

Was Thomas Jefferson opposed to religion?

No, he attended church every Sunday by riding horseback from the White House to the Capital building where a Christian Church service was held on Sundays.

Question 29

Who was John Jay?

John Jay was the 1st Chief Justice of the Supreme Court.

Question 30

What important statement did John Jay make about the importance of learning the Constitution and the Bill of Rights?

He said, "it is time for every American to learn what is in the Constitution and the Bill of Rights. By knowing our rights, we will know when they are violated and be better prepared to defend these rights for future generations."

Question 31

Who is known as the Father of the Constitution?

James Madison was known as the Father of the Constitution because of his key role in drafting the Constitution and including three branches of government.

Question 32

What are the three branches of our government?

The three branches of our government consist of the legislative branch, the executive branch, and the judicial branch.

Question 33

Why did our Founding Father's want 3 branches of the government?

The Founding Fathers wanted 3 branches of the government for checks and balances to limit power by any one branch.

Question 34

Who was the 1st President of the United States and known as the Father of our country?

George Washington was the 1st President and known as the Father of our country.

Question 35

What was the name of the war that was fought by the colonists to free them from the British?

The American Revolutionary War was the war that was fought by the colonists to free themselves from British rule.

Question 36

Who was the General that lead the American Revolutionary Army against the British?

General George Washington was the general that led the colonists in the American Revolutionary War to free themselves from British rule.

Question 37

What are the names of the 13 colonies in America that were under British rule?

The 13 colonies under British rule were New Hampshire, New York, Massachusetts, Connecticut, Rhode Island, Pennsylvania, New Jersey, Delaware, Maryland, Virginia, North Carolina, South Carolina and Georgia.

Question 38

Who was the Vice President under George Washington who later became the 2nd President of the United States of America?

John Adams was Vice President under George Washington and became the 2nd President of the United States.

Question 39

What was the name of the document sent by the colonists to King George III to protest their unfair treatment?

The document sent by the colonists to King George III containing 27 grievances was called the Declaration of Independence.

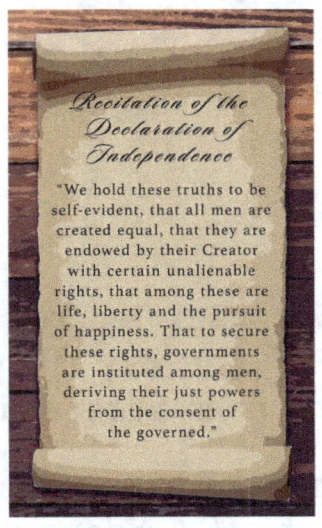

Question 40

What is a grievance?

A grievance is a complaint about unfair treatment, injury, or a violation of rights.

Question 41

What day and year was the Declaration of Independence signed?

The Declaration of Independence was signed on July 4, 1776.

Question 42

What holiday does America celebrate to remember the day they declared independence from Great Britain?

The holiday America celebrates to remember their independence from Great Britain is the 4th of July.

Question 43

Did King George III ever listen to the complaints of the colonists and decide to treat them fairly?

No, King George III did not listen to the colonists and treat them fairly but instead they were treated even worse.

Question 44

What was the final spark that caused a point of no return and the beginning of the American Revolutionary War?

The final breaking point occurred during the battles of Lexington and Concord on April 19th, 1775. The British had been making an attempt to seize colonial military supplies and arrest patriot leaders.

Question 45

Who did the colonists choose to lead their Continental Army against the British?

The man chosen to lead the Continental Army against the British was General George Washington.

Question 46

After the war was won with the British, why did the new free and independent states need to meet in Philadelphia, Pennsylvania?

The new states decided to meet because they discovered the government was too weak under the existing Articles of Confederation.

Question 47

What were some of the problems the states were having?

The states had no power to:

1. Tax

2. Pay debts

3. Fund an army

4. Regulate trade

5. Print money that could be used in every state.

6. Have a court system that could settle disputes between states.

Question 48

What does ratify mean?

To ratify means to sign into law.

Question 49

What state and year did the 9th state ratify the Constitution?

The state of New Hampshire ratified the Constitution on June 21, 1788.

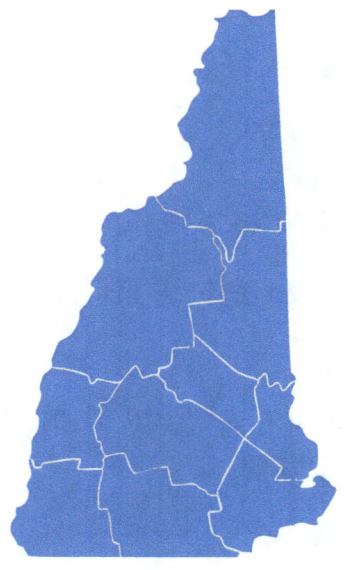

Question 50

When do we celebrate Constitution Day?

We celebrate Constitution Day on September 17 because the Constitution was first signed on September 17, 1787

Question 51

When the Constitution was signed, there were only two parts. Name these parts.

The two parts to the Constitution were the Preamble and the 7 Articles.

Question 52

Was there a Bill of Rights in the original Constitution?

No, there was no Bill of Rights in the original Constitution.

Question 53

Who pushed so hard for the Bill of Rights to be added to the Constitution that he became known as the Father of the Bill of Rights?

George Mason pushed so hard for a Bill of Rights to be added to the Constitution that he became known as the Father of the Bill of Rights.

Question 54

What are the three parts to the Constitution?

The three parts to the Constitution are the Preamble , the 7 Articles , and the 27 Amendments.

Question 55

When the first Congress met, who proposed the first Amendments to the Constitution?

James Madison proposed the first Amendments to the Constitution of which the first 10 became known as the Bill of Rights.

Question 56

Who became the 3rd president of the United States and what is he mostly known for?

Thomas Jefferson became the 3rd President of the United States and is mostly known for drafting the Declaration of Independence.

Founding Fathers
Hall of Fame

Founding Father
George Washington

George Washington was the first President of the United States and is often known as the Father of our country. He was the head of the Continental Army during the American Revolutionary War and was known for his strong moral character.

See: George Washington's Thanksgiving Proclamation pages 89-93.

Founding Father

Benjamin Franklin

Benjamin Franklin was one of the Founding Fathers of our country helping to draft the Declaration of Independence and the Constitution. He was also a scientist, printer, writer, inventor, and diplomat. He was the first Postmaster General of the United States and founded the University of Pennsylvania. He also helped start the first volunteer fire department in Philadelphia, Pennsylvania.

Founding Father
John Adams

John Adams was the second President of the United States. He was a key figure in the American Revolution , a persuasive and brilliant lawyer from Massachusetts and one of the Founding Fathers. He helped draft the Declaration of Independence and was one of the signers.

Founding Father
Thomas Jefferson

Thomas Jefferson was the third president of the United States, serving from 1801 to 1809. He's best known for the writing the Declaration of Independence in 1776 and being a big advocate for individual rights. He was also interested in farming, architecture, science, and education. He founded the University of Virginia and even designed its campus. His huge estate is called Monticello.

*** While Jefferson was President, he wrote a letter to the Danbury Baptists on January 1, 1802. The churches in the Danbury Baptist Association were worried about their religious freedoms under the new government. Jefferson reassured them that the first Amendment protects people's rights to practice their faith without interference from the government. He used the expression that there was a "wall of separation between the Church and State."

The phrase "wall of separation" is nowhere in any of our founding documents, but only in the letter that Jefferson wrote in 1802 while he was President.

Founding Father

John Jay

John Jay was one of the Founding Fathers of the United States and the first Chief Justice of the Supreme Court serving from 1789 to 1795. He co-authored the Federalist Papers to persuade states to ratify the Constitution. He also helped negotiate the Treaty of Paris, officially ending the American Revolutionary War.

Founding Father
Alexander Hamilton

Alexander Hamilton was one of the Founding Fathers coming to America from the Caribbean. He became George Washington's right-hand man during the American Revolutionary War, and after the war became the first Secretary of the Treasury, pushing for a strong national bank and financial system.

Founding Father
James Madison

James Madison became the first Secretary of State serving under Thomas Jefferson. He became the fourth President of the United States serving from 1809 to 1817. He's often called the Father of the Constitution because of his huge role in drafting and pushing the Bill of Rights and the idea of checks and balances in the government.

Founding Father
Benjamin Rush

Benjamin Rush was a Founding Father and signer of the Declaration of Independence. He served as Surgeon general in the Continental Army. He's often accredited as the Father of American medicine because of his many contributions to medicine and better treatment for the mentally ill. He was a strong advocate for abolition of slavery.

It was noted in newspapers at the time of Benjamin Rush's death that Founding Fathers and other leaders ranked him as one of the three most notable individuals of his time along with George Washington and Benjamin Franklin.

Father of the Bill of Rights

George Mason

George Mason was one of the Founding Fathers and known for drafting the Virginia Declaration of Rights. He was a huge influencer in the Bill of Rights that was added to the Constitution during the 1st Congress of the United States. He is often called the Father of the Bill of Rights because he would not sign the Constitution when others signed it in 1787. He felt it needed a Bill of Rights to protect individuals and was suspicious of a strong central government.

Bill of Rights

The Bill of Rights

The first 10 amendments to the Constitution are called the Bill of Rights and they were ratified December 15th, 1791.

Amendment I.

Congress shall make no law respecting an establishment of religion or prohibiting the free exercise thereof; or abridging the freedom of speech, or of the press, or the right of the people peaceably to assemble, and to petition the Government for a redress of grievances.

Amendment II.

A well-regulated Militia, being necessary to the security of a free State, the right of the people to keep and bear Arms, shall not be infringed.

Amendment III.

No Soldier shall, in time of peace be quartered in any house, without the consent of the Owner, nor in time of war, but in a manner to be prescribed by law.

Amendment IV.

The right of the people to be secure in their persons, houses, papers, and effects, against unreasonable searches and seizures, shall not be violated, and no Warrants shall issue, but upon probable cause, supported by Oath or affirmation, and particularly describing the places to be searched, and the person or things to be seized.

Amendment V.

No person shall be held to answer for a capital, or otherwise infamous crime, unless on a presentment or indictment of a Grand Jury, except in cases arising in the land or naval forces, or in the Militia, when in actual service in time of War or public danger; nor shall any person be subject for the same offense to be twice put in jeopardy of life or limb; nor shall be compelled in any criminal case to be a witness against himself, nor be deprived

of life, liberty, or property, without due process of law; nor shall private property be taken for public use, without just compensation.

Amendment VI.

In all criminal prosecutions, the accused shall enjoy the right to a speedy and public trial, by an impartial jury of the State and district wherein the crime shall have been committed, which district shall have been previously ascertained by law, and to be informed of the nature and cause of the accusation; to be confronted with the witnesses against him; to have compulsory process for obtaining witnesses in his favor, and to have the assistance of counsel for his defense.

Amendment VII.

In Suits at common law, where the value in controversy shall exceed twenty dollars, the right of trial by jury shall be preserved, and no fact tried by a jury shall be otherwise reexamined in any Court of the United States, than according to the rules of the common law.

Amendment VIII.

Excessive bail shall not be required, nor excessive fines imposed, nor cruel and unusual punishments inflicted.

Amendment IX.

The enumeration in the Constitution, of certain rights, shall not be construed to deny or disparage others retained by the people.

Amendment X.

The powers not delegated to the United States by the Constitution, nor prohibited by it to the States, are reserved to the States respectively, or to the people. [1]

Letter To The
Danbury Baptists

Letter from Thomas Jefferson to the Danbury Baptists

To messers. Nehemiah Dodge, Ephraim Robbins, & Stephen S. Nelson, a committee of the Danbury Baptist Association in the state of Connecticut.

Gentlemen

The affectionate sentiments of esteem and approbation which you are so good as to express towards me, on behalf of the Danbury Baptist association, give me the highest satisfaction. My duties dictate a faithful and zealous pursuit of the interests of my constituents, & in proportion as they are persuaded of my fidelity to those duties, the discharge of them becomes more and more pleasing.

Believing with you that religion is a matter which lies solely between Man & his God, that he owes account to none other for his faith or his worship, that the legitimate powers of government reach actions only, & not opinions, I contemplate with sovereign reverence that act of the whole

American people which declared that their legislature should "make no law respecting an establishment of religion, or prohibiting the free exercise thereof," thus building a wall of separation between Church & State. Adhering to this expression of the supreme will of the nation in behalf of the rights of conscience, I shall see with sincere satisfaction the progress of those sentiments which tend to restore to man all his natural rights, convinced he has no natural right in opposition to his social duties.

I reciprocate your kind prayers for the protection & blessing of the common father and creator of man, and tender you for yourselves & your religious association, assurances of my high respect & esteem.

Th Jefferson
Jan. 1. 1802. [2]

George Washington's Thanksgiving Proclamation

President George Washington's Thanksgiving Proclamation of 1789

(As originally written using early English.)

A Proclamation

Whereas it is the duty of all nations to acknowledge the Providence of Almighty God, to obey his will, to be grateful for his benefits, and humbly to implore his protection and favor-and Whereas both Houses of Congress have by their Joint Committee requested me "to recommend to the People of the United States a day of public Thanksgiving and prayer to be observed by acknowledging with grateful hearts the many signal favors of Almighty God, especially by affording them an opportunity peaceably to establish a form of government for their safety and happiness."

Now therefore I do recommend and assign Thursday the 26th day of November next to be devoted by the People of these States to the service of that great and

glorious Being, who is the beneficent Author of all the good that was, that is, or that will be-that we may then all unite in rendering unto him our sincere and humble thanks-for his kind care and protection of the People of this country previous to their becoming a Nation-for the signal and manifold mercies, and the favorable interpositions of his great Providence, which we experienced in the course and conclusion of the late war-for the great degree of tranquility, union, and plenty, which we have since enjoyed-for the peaceable and rational manner in which we have been enable to establish constitutions of government for our safety and happiness, and particularly the national One now lately instituted, for the civil and religious liberty with which we are blessed and the means we have of acquiring and diffusing useful knowledge; And in general for all the great and various favors which he hath been pleased to confer upon us.

And also that we may then unite in most humbly offering our prayers and supplications to the great Lord and Ruler of Nations and to seek him to pardon our national and other transgressions-to enable us all, whether in public or private stations, to perform our several and relative duties properly and punctually-to render our national government a blessing to all the people, by constantly being a government of wise, just, and constitutional laws, discreetly and faithfully executed and obeyed-to protect and guide all Sovereigns and Nations (especially such as have shown kindness unto us) and to bless them with good government, peace, and concord-to promote the knowledge and practice of true religion and virtue, and the increase of science among them and Us-and generally to grant unto all mankind such a degree of temporal prosperity as he alone knows to be best.

Given under my hand at the City of New York the third day of October in the year of our Lord 1789.

Go. Washington [3]

<u>Endnotes</u>

1. United States Bill of Rights, proposed by Congress, September 25th, 1789, ratified December 15th, 1791, National Archives and records administration, Washington, DC,https:// www.archives. gov/foundingdocs/bill-of-rights. The first 10 Amendments to the U.S. Constitution, drafted to protect individual liberties and limit federal power, were introduced by James Madison and ratified by the states following debates over the need for explicit guarantee of rights.

2. Thomas Jefferson to the Danbury Baptist Association, January 1st, 1802, manuscript division, Library of Congress, Washington, DC, https://www.loc. gov/item/mtjbib010841/. Jefferson responds in a letter to the concerns of the Danbury Baptist Association about their freedom of religious liberty in Connecticut.

3. George Washington, Thanksgiving Proclamation, October 3, 1789 issued in

response to a congressional request for a National Day of Thanksgiving and Prayer. See "Transcript of President George Washington's Thanksgiving proclamation," Smithsonian institute, https://www. si.edu.

Current Products List

All Products are available from our web site:
https://Karen-Moran.com

Large Orders Contact:
info@patriotcountrypublishers.com

Bill of Rights Full Packet

Includes paperback book *(large print)*, color posters, (laminated option) letter size *(8 1/2 x 11")*.

Includes all 10 Amendments and coloring pages.

U.S. Constitution for Kids

Original Foundational Book

Paperback book, large print, 185 pages, $17.76

Discounts available for large orders.

Contact: info@patriotcountrypublishers.com

U.S. Constitution for Kids
(for use in schools)

Book 1 in the Founding Documents for Kids series.

Paperback book, large print, $17.76

Discounts available for large orders.

Contact: info@patriotcountrypublishers.com

Bill of Rights for Kids
(for use in schools)

Book 2 in the Founding Documents for Kids series.

Paperback book, large print, 115 pages, $16.99

Discounts available for large orders.

Contact: info@patriotcountrypublishers.com

Declaration of Independence
for Kids
(for use in schools)

Book 3 in the Founding Documents for Kids series.

Paperback book, large print, $16.99

Discounts available for large orders.

Contact: info@patriotcountrypublishers.com

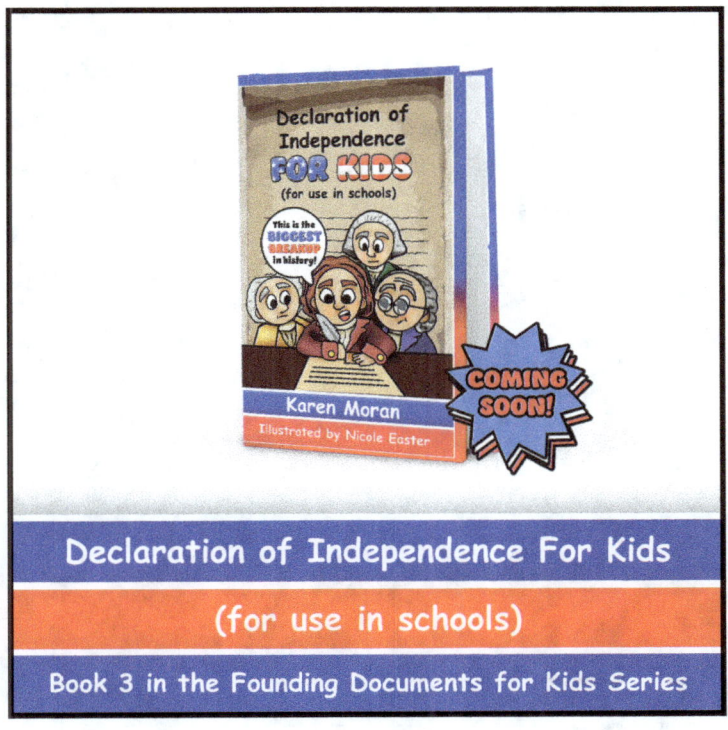

www.ingramcontent.com/pod-product-compliance
Lightning Source LLC
Chambersburg PA
CBHW071329130626
46556CB00004B/1809